D0426191

May His Face

Shine

upon You

Books by Susie Larson:

Your Beautiful Purpose

Blessings for the Evening

Blessings for the Morning

Your Sacred Yes

Your Powerful Prayers

Blessings for the Soul

Blessings for Morning and Evening

Bountiful Blessings

Fully Alive

Prevail

Prepare Him Room

May His Face *Shine* upon You

90 BIBLICAL BLESSINGS
FOR MOTHER
AND CHILD

SUSIE LARSON

BETHANYHOUSE

a division of Baker Publishing Group
Minneapolis, Minnesota

© 2022 by Susie Larson

Published by Bethany House Publishers
11400 Hampshire Avenue South
Bloomington, Minnesota 55438
www.bethanyhouse.com

Bethany House Publishers is a division of
Baker Publishing Group, Grand Rapids, Michigan

Printed in China

All rights reserved. No part of this publication may be reproduced, stored in a retrieval
system, or transmitted in any form or by any means—for example, electronic, photocopy,
recording—without the prior written permission of the publisher. The only exception is brief
quotations in printed reviews.

Library of Congress Cataloging-in-Publication Data
Names: Larson, Susie, 1962– author.
Title: May his face shine upon you : 90 biblical blessings for mother and child / Susie Larson.
Description: Minneapolis, MN : Bethany House Publishers, a division of Baker Publishing
    Group, [2021] | Includes index.
Identifiers: LCCN 2021029291 | ISBN 9780764238543 | ISBN 9781493435739 (ebook)
Subjects: LCSH: Mothers—Prayers and devotions. | Children—Prayers and devotions.
Classification: LCC BV283.M7 L37 2021 | DDC 242/.6431—dc23
LC record available at https://lccn.loc.gov/2021029291

Unless otherwise indicated, Scripture quotations are from the Holy Bible, New Living Translation, copyright © 1996, 2004, 2015 by Tyndale House Foundation. Used by permission of
Tyndale House Publishers, Inc., Carol Stream, Illinois 60188. All rights reserved.

Scripture quotations labeled HCSB are from the Holman Christian Standard Bible®, copyright
© 1999, 2000, 2002, 2003, 2009 by Holman Bible Publishers. Used by permission. Holman Christian Standard Bible®, Holman CSB®, and HCSB® are federally registered trade-
marks of Holman Bible Publishers.

Scripture quotations labeled MSG are taken from THE MESSAGE, copyright © 1993, 2002,
2018 by Eugene H. Peterson. Used by permission of NavPress. All rights reserved. Represented by Tyndale House Publishers, Inc.

Scripture quotations labeled NIV are from THE HOLY BIBLE, NEW INTERNATIONAL VER-
SION®, NIV® Copyright © 1973, 1978, 1984, 2011 by Biblica, Inc.® Used by permission. All
rights reserved worldwide.

Scripture quotations labeled NKJV are from the New King James Version®. Copyright © 1982
by Thomas Nelson. Used by permission. All rights reserved.

Scripture quotations labeled TLB are from The Living Bible, copyright © 1971. Used by permission of Tyndale House Publishers, Inc., Carol Stream, Illinois 60188. All rights reserved.

Scripture quotations labeled THE VOICE are from The Voice Bible Copyright © 2012 Thomas
Nelson, Inc. The Voice™ translation © 2012 Ecclesia Bile Society All rights reserved.

Cover design by Jennifer Parker

Author is represented by The Steve Laube Agency

Baker Publishing Group publications use paper produced from sustainable forestry practices
and post-consumer waste whenever possible.

22 23 24 25 26 27 28   7 6 5 4 3 2 1

To my dear grandchildren—
the ones I enjoy now,
and the ones I've yet to meet.
May God's hand of blessing
be upon you always.

TABLE OF CONTENTS
by Subject

Amazing grace

24

Be strong and courageous

3, 18, 23, 27, 51, 73, 76, 82, 85, 89

Believe in God's big plans for you

17, 19, 29, 40, 56, 76, 89, 90

Bullies

16, 39, 69

Chosen by God

1, 32, 59

Delivered from sin

8, 12, 24, 33, 61, 80, 82

Eyes on Jesus

22, 38, 69, 78, 80, 83

Facing the enemy

5, 39, 73, 77, 89

Fear

9, 14, 18, 31, 36, 41, 51, 63, 85

Forgiveness

8, 12, 24, 33, 61, 80, 82

Freedom from others' opinions

41, 48, 69

Friends

47, 60, 72, 88

Future

26, 42, 49, 57, 64

God delights in you

35, 65, 74, 75, 81

God provides

57, 79, 81

God-given assignment

3, 17, 28, 29, 50, 74, 86

God's faithfulness
33, 57

God's favor and power
5, 38, 40, 51

God's love
1, 2, 14, 32, 36, 37, 61, 64, 74, 75, 81, 85, 88, 89

God's plan for you
3, 5, 11, 74, 86

God's power to heal
4, 15, 34

God's power to restore
4, 15, 34, 46, 53, 68, 78, 82

God's protection
1, 14, 20, 51, 79

Gratitude/ thankfulness
11, 44, 49, 52, 60, 63

How God grows us (maturity)
7, 50, 72

Humility
67

Joy
25, 47, 52, 62

Knowing right from wrong
3, 13, 72, 77, 83

Leadership
16

Let God lead
3

Love your enemies
61

Peace of God
43

Perseverance
66, 71, 84

Powerful prayers
6, 45, 55, 58, 90

Power of the gospel
21

Promises of God
35, 42, 58, 59, 86

Rest and replenishment
2, 10, 20, 70, 87

Sadness
4, 46, 67, 84

Sharing your faith
21

Spiritual warfare
23, 27, 39, 73

Trust in God
54, 76

Wisdom
30, 77

Worry
9, 31, 88

You be you (a work in progress)
8, 65

INTRODUCTION

Jesus loves you more than your precious heart could ever fathom. And He loves your treasured child even more than you do. Yet we have a very real enemy who isn't out to just poke fun at us; he aims to steal, kill, and destroy all that's beautiful and blossoming in our lives. You, no doubt, remember the first time someone said something to you that pierced your heart and hurt your soul. Maybe you don't recall what they said, but you do remember how you felt afterward. Words are powerful. They bring death or life; discouragement or encouragement; hurt or healing.

Jesus merely spoke, and the heavens were created.

As believers, filled with the Spirit of the living God, our words—especially when we're speaking God's Words—are fused with power, purpose, and potential. We don't have to sit idly by and let the enemy have his way in our lives and our children's lives. We can dare to rise up, receive by faith what God says about us, believe it in our hearts until it changes us, and then lovingly pass these blessings on to our children. In the Jewish culture, spoken blessings were a regular part of family life. What if biblical blessings made a comeback? Not wishful thinking. Not positive thoughts. But true, biblical exhortations right out of the promises from Scripture.

The Bible says that faith comes by hearing, and hearing by the Word of God. It is my prayer that you not whip through these short readings, but that you pause long enough to ponder them, meditate on them, and use them as conversation starters with your children. Oh, that they (and you) may know the love of God in a way that changes you!

We live in a world where negative words have become the norm. May your family become so acquainted with God's love and His promises that your home becomes a city on a hill, a light that points others to a God who loves them.

With great love and affection,

Susie Larson

1 Step by Step with God

Blessing for Mom

May God surround you with a strong sense of His great love for you! May you live every day with the expectancy that He is moving in your life. May the Word of God come alive to you in a way you've never experienced. And may your prayers take on a whole new level of power and faith. You are His child, and He is with you every step of the way. Be blessed with deep rest this evening.

Blessing for Child

Do you know how much God loves you? I hope you do, and that every day you remember that He is taking care of you. Listen to what the Bible says, ask God to watch over you, and trust that He's on your side! You are God's child, and He's with you every step of the way. Get a great night's sleep resting in God's arms.

But as for me, it is *good* to be near God. I have made the Sovereign LORD my *refuge*; I will tell of all your deeds.

PSALM 73:28 NIV

2 When You Need Rest and Peace

Blessing for Mom

By God's grace, may you eliminate hurry and worry from your life. May you instead slow your pace and turn your face to the One who loves, saves, redeems, and restores everything about you. Instead of grabbing for yourself, may you pause and wait and see how God provides and cares for you. May you enter into a new season where you know God's rest, His pace, and His provision like you've never known before. He's for you and with you in ways you can't even imagine!

Blessing for Child

Close your eyes. Take a deep breath. Relax. May God help you slow down and be thankful for everything He's given you. Remember how much He loves you and wants to take care of you. He wants you to sleep well, and always remember that He's ready to give you everything you need. He is cheering for you every step of the way!

No eye has *seen*,
no ear has *heard*, and
no mind has *imagined*
what God has prepared for
those who *love* him.

1 CORINTHIANS 2:9

When You're Looking for Direction

Blessing for Mom

May God give you absolute clarity and divine discernment so you can see things as they are, and not as they seem. May He keep you far from accusing tongues and protect you from being wrongly assessed. May you have the backbone and conviction to stand up for what is true, and to stand back when God wants to fight for you. May God give you laser-like focus to tend to your God-given assignment. May He grant you empowering grace to flourish where He has placed you. May your pure heart and firm faith keep you steady on the path ahead of you. These things are yours because you belong to Him.

Blessing for Child

Sometimes it's hard to tell the difference between good things and bad things. May God help you always know which way you should go and what you should do, and may He keep you from getting in trouble for things that weren't your fault. May He help you be brave and stand up for what's right, but also let you know when you can relax and let Him do the fighting for you. God loves you and has wonderful things for you to do. You belong to Him.

All *praise* to God, the Father of
our Lord Jesus Christ,
who has blessed us with every
spiritual blessing in the
heavenly realms because we
are *united* with Christ.

EPHESIANS 1:3

When Disappointments Come

Blessing for Mom

May you begin to see your setbacks as temporary, your delays as detours, and your heartbreaks as opportunities to experience God's precious, powerful healing. And in the meantime, may God give you glimpses of glory, insights into His good plan for you. Be assured that God has never left your side; He'll never let you go. May God help you see with supernatural insight so that you won't be deceived by the enemy of your soul, or by your past painful filters, or by your fears of the future. In fact, right here—in this place—may your divine perspective hugely inspire your faith steps. You are mighty in God, and He is mighty in you.

Blessing for Child

Even when sad things happen, God still loves you and is right by your side. He is so powerful and has big plans for your life. He'll never let you go. Don't be tricked by the devil or be scared of things that might happen later. God is strong enough to take care of you and will give you the strength you need to face anything.

"Don't be afraid!"
Elisha told him. "For there are
more on our side than on theirs!"
Then Elisha prayed,
"O LORD, open his *eyes*
and let him *see*!" The LORD
opened the young man's eyes,
and when he looked up, he
saw that the hillside around
Elisha was filled with horses
and *chariots of fire.*

2 KINGS 6:16–17

5

God Is Moving

Blessing for Mom

May you dare to believe that God is moving in your life, because He is. He makes all things new. And He intends to dismantle the schemes of the enemy. Will you trust Him? May your next steps be faith steps and your next words be faith words. May you embrace a joyful heart, not because of what your eyes see, but because of what your heart knows: God is good, He is for you, and He WILL NOT fail you. Have a blessed day.

Blessing for Child

God is doing something big in your life. Believe it! The devil has tricks up his sleeve, but God is smarter and won't let him win. Trust in God, go where He wants you to go, and say what He wants you to say. Smile inside because you know that God is good and He's got your back. Have a great day!

He who was seated on the throne said, "I am making everything *new*!" Then he said, "Write this down, for these words are *trustworthy* and true."

REVELATION 21:5 NIV

6 Prayer Changes Things

Blessing for Mom

May you begin to see with Spirit-eyes all the ways God is moving because of your prayers. May you begin to hear with heavenly ears the song heaven sings over you. May you begin to know—on a deeper level—how important and precious your faith is to God. And may you begin to know that God's promises are absolutely true, and live accordingly. God loves you and loves how He made you. A happy and blessed day to you!

Blessing for Child

Did you know your prayers move God's heart? God listens to what you say and moves in a way that's best for you because you ask Him to! In fact, right now, Jesus is talking and singing to God about you! I hope your heart can feel and know the great things God's doing even when your eyes and ears can't see it or hear it. Trusting in God is so important. He never lies, and He loves you so much without you even trying. Have a wonderful day!

It is good to *praise* the LORD
and make music to your name,
O Most High, *proclaiming*
your love in the morning and
your faithfulness at night.

PSALM 92:1–2 NIV

7 Filled to Overflowing

Blessing for Mom

May you experience increase in every way. May your capacity to know the heights of God's love grow exponentially. May your understanding of the depths of His faithfulness grow continually. May your belief in your divine value deepen tremendously. And in the days ahead, may your willingness to trust God with every detail of your life change profoundly. You are deeply loved, deeply called, and profoundly cared for. May you live out of this truth! Walk in humble confidence today.

Blessing for Child

I'm rooting for you to get bigger and stronger and more able to do all the things God has for you to do! And along the way, may you know how much God loves you and treasures you. I hope you keep trusting in God more and more every day and that you are brave because you know how much He cares for you.

I pray that you, being *rooted* and *established* in love, may have power, together with all the Lord's holy people, to grasp how wide and long and high and deep is the *love of Christ*, and to know this love that surpasses knowledge—that you may be filled to the measure of all the *fullness* of God.

EPHESIANS 3:17–19 NIV

8 Free to Be You

Blessing for Mom

May you find a new freedom in being the YOU God created you to be! May you be comfortable in your own skin, excited about your own story, and at peace with your own past because Christ has redeemed every part of you. May you break free from condemnation, may you walk away from toxic influences, and may you put fear under your feet. Let faith fill your heart. Do not give people the power that belongs to God alone. He loves you. He is strong. And He'll keep you strong till the end. Have a faith-filled day today!

Blessing for Child

God made you special! He wants you to be confident about being exactly who He made you to be! Sure, you're not perfect—no one is, everyone messes up at times—but God forgives you, and so do I. Don't be scared, and don't hang around people who try to make you do things you know are wrong. God loves you. He's strong, and He will help you be strong too!

Now you have every spiritual *gift* you need as you eagerly wait for the return of our Lord Jesus Christ. He will keep you *strong* to the end so that you will be free from *all* blame on the day when our Lord Jesus Christ returns.

1 CORINTHIANS 1:7–8

9 Release Your Cares

Blessing for Mom

May God himself surround you with His tender mercies and grace today. May He heal your soul so you can live by faith. Where you once reacted out of your insecurities, may you respond in faith, knowing you possess all in Christ. Where you once white-knuckled your worries, may you release every care to Him and lift your hands in praise. You are not made for this world. You are only passing through. Live as the divinely loved and called soul you are!

Blessing for Child

I hope you can sense how much God cares for you today. I know you sometimes feel shy or weak or scared, but I want you to know that you don't have to be any of these things because you are strong in Jesus. We all worry sometimes, but I hope you know you can give your worries to Him. Jesus will take good care of you. He'll take your fears and make you brave. Live your life believing God loves you. Get excited about your future. You'll enjoy heaven with Him someday!

So we *fix* our eyes not on what is seen, but on what is *unseen*, since what is seen is temporary, but what is unseen is *eternal*.

2 CORINTHIANS 4:18 NIV

10

Simplify and Refresh

Blessing for Mom

May God inspire you to tackle a project you've been putting off. May He motivate you to clean out the clutter and simplify your surroundings. May He refresh your weary soul and renew your tired mind. And in every way, may your soul be restored, your mind renewed, and your spirit at peace. He leads you by still waters; follow Him there. Be revived and refreshed this day!

Blessing for Child

You've got a big job to do, so don't put it off! God will make you strong and energetic so you can get it done. I hope that even when you have big plans, you feel rest and peace, and that you know God is holding your hand every step of the way.

May the God of *hope* fill you
with all joy and peace as you
trust in him, so that you
may overflow with hope by the
power of the Holy Spirit.

ROMANS 15:13 NIV

11

Sow Generously

Blessing for Mom

May you choose joy this day! May you look for and count your many blessings. May you sow generously for a future harvest. May you trust God with the seeds you have in the ground. And may you add faith to every deed, knowing that God multiplies what we sow in faith. Have an abundantly joyful day today!

Blessing for Child

Be joyful because of all the things God has given you! Don't pout or wish for what somebody else has. God has everything you need and more. God wants to bless you and bless the world through you! He will take your efforts and grow them into huge blessings that will surprise you and bless others! Have a wonderful, joyful day!

Give, and it will be *given* to you. A good measure, pressed down, shaken together and running over, will be *poured* into your lap. For with the measure you use, it will be *measured* to you.

LUKE 6:38 NIV

A Brand-New You

Blessing for Mom

May God's opinion matter far more to you than man's opinion. May His dreams for you speak louder than your fears. May His forgiveness wash over every sin from your past. And may you rise up in the morning with the knowledge that He's made you brand-new, through and through. No spot or stain on you! Rest well tonight.

Blessing for Child

God thinks you're terrific, and that's more important than what anyone else thinks about you! Rest your head on the pillow tonight knowing that God loves you and is cheering for you. Tomorrow is a brand-new day. I want you to know that God forgives you; you are clean and perfect in His eyes. You can wake up tomorrow with a joyful heart. Have a good night's sleep!

There is no condemnation for those who *belong* to Christ Jesus. And because you belong to him, the power of the *life-giving Spirit* has freed you from the power of sin that leads to death. . . . The Spirit of God, who raised Jesus from the dead, *lives* in you. And just as God raised Christ Jesus from the dead, he will give life to your mortal bodies by this same Spirit living within you.

ROMANS 8:1–2, 11

13

Seeing and Hearing God

Blessing for Mom

May God bless your eyes so you begin to see everyone and everything redemptively. May God bless your ears so you'll hear only words consistent with His voice and His song over your life. May God bless your heart so that you may be a wellspring of life for others. And may God bless your hands and feet so that you may tend to His business during your time on earth. Your life matters deeply to Him. Sleep well tonight.

Blessing for Child

May you see things the way God sees them—He can even bring good things out of bad things. He can turn anything around! May you be careful what you listen to and determine to only hear the stuff God wants you to hear—beautiful words and songs and anything that fills you up with joy and strength. Then you'll be able to do all the things God has for you to do. You are so important to God! Good night, my love.

Your eyes are *blessed* because they do *see*, and your ears because they do *hear*!

MATTHEW 13:16 HCSB

God's Powerful Love

Blessing for Mom

May God fine-tune your spiritual ears so you hear heaven's song above the chaos and the noise. May you rest in the knowledge that God is in control and will have the last say when it's all said and done. Though the elements rage and the enemy taunts, God is the One who fights for you, and He will win for you. He loves you with power and with passion. May His kingdom come and His will be done everywhere you place your feet today. Have a powerful day in Him!

Blessing for Child

May God help you see and hear all of the ways He's working all around you—even though others may miss Him. He's in control. We can trust Him, even when bad things happen. There may be a scary storm outside, or other kids might be mean to you, but God is right there with you through it all. In the end He wins every fight, and He's on your side. Have a great day with God!

The LORD your God is *with* you, the Mighty Warrior who *saves*. He will take great delight in you; in his love he will no longer rebuke you, but will *rejoice* over you with singing.

ZEPHANIAH 3:17 NIV

A Healthy Rhythm

Blessing for Mom

May the Lord establish in you a healthy, divine rhythm of life. May He strengthen you in mind, body, and spirit. Where you're broken, may He restore; where you're weary, may He refresh; where you're fearful, may He revive faith. May your coming days be far more blessed than your former days. Sleep well tonight. There will be new mercies waiting for you in the morning.

Blessing for Child

May God help you grow up to be strong and smart and wise. And may He always heal your hurts—whether it's your body or your feelings that are hurting. When you're scared, may God make you brave, and may your life keep getting better and better! Have a great night's sleep, and may tomorrow be amazing!

Come to Me, all of you who
are weary and burdened,
and I will give you *rest*.

MATTHEW 11:28 HCSB

16 Your Influence Matters

Blessing for Mom

In the days ahead, may you die to the power of others' opinions and instead live out of the relentless, abundant love God has for you. As people become more cruel and careless with their opinions, may you become more loving and discerning with yours. May you speak with precision, pray with power, and stand in courage. Your life and influence matter deeply in this desperate world. Lean in and learn everything you can from the One who loves you deeply and intends to use you greatly.

Blessing for Child

Sometimes people can be mean. They might call you names or say things that hurt your feelings. Shake it off! Instead of being mean right back to them, say kind things, and always be ready to stand up for others who are being picked on too. That's what brave kids do. God loves you so much and has big plans for you.

When she speaks, her
words are *wise*, and
she gives instructions
with *kindness*.

PROVERBS 31:26

Stepping Out

Blessing for Mom

May God inspire you to achieve a goal that He puts in your heart. May He stir up faith as you step up and step out. May He give you fresh conviction and discipline to say no to lesser things so you can say yes to His best plan for you. May the wind of the Holy Spirit fill your sail and take you to a new, inspired place. And tonight, sleep well.

Blessing for Child

Do you have a dream about being able to do something big? May God help you get it done! Sometimes you have to say no to things that get in the way—maybe spending less time on things like video games or TV—so you have more time to follow your big dream. May God give you strength and energy along the way! And in the meantime, have a good night's sleep.

Since we are *surrounded* by
such a huge crowd of witnesses
to the life of *faith*, let us
strip off every weight that slows
us down, especially the sin that
so easily trips us up. And let
us run with *endurance* the
race God has set before us.

HEBREWS 12:1

18

Peace to Your Storm

Blessing for Mom

May Jesus speak peace to your soul and calm to your storm. May you sense His nearness even when the winds blow. May you know His joy and strength from the top of your head to the tips of your toes. May the hope He stirs in your heart cause you to live with a holy expectancy and trust that this storm, too, shall pass. And in the days ahead, may His very real love for you compel you to dance in the rain before the sun breaks through. He goes before you, He's got your back, and He's there, just around the bend. He'll never forsake you. Trust Him today!

Blessing for Child

Sometimes bad things happen and we get scared. That's normal, but God can make you brave! May He give you joy and courage from your head to your toes. Instead of hiding from the storm, you'll be dancing in the rain, waiting for the sun to come back out! God is always with you—you can count on it!

He got up, *rebuked* the
wind and said to the waves,
"Quiet! Be still!"
Then the wind died down
and it was completely *calm*.

MARK 4:39 NIV

19

Crazy Faith Steps

Blessing for Mom

May you—above all else—see yourself as someone Jesus loves. May His affection for you heal you in the deepest ways and inspire you like nothing else ever has. May His saving grace and enabling power compel you to dream with Him, believe in Him, and take crazy faith steps because of Him. May every lesser voice and every lying circumstance fall by the wayside so that all you hear is His voice in your ear, saying, "This is the way, walk in it." Nobody can save, heal, redeem, and refresh like Jesus. Walk intimately with Him today.

Blessing for Child

Think big! Jesus loves you so much, and He can help you accomplish the big dreams He's put in your heart. May you always listen to what He's saying and ignore the people who tell you to do something else. Walk with Jesus, and hold His hand. He's got you!

Now to him who is *able*
to do immeasurably more
than all we ask or imagine,
according to his *power* that
is at work *within* us.

EPHESIANS 3:20 NIV

20 Pause, Rest, Reflect

Blessing for Mom

May you be mindful to pause regularly and reflect on the many ways God has come through for you. This will strengthen your heart. May you cultivate a heart that knows how to rest in God alone. This will nourish your soul. As you look to Jesus and remember His faithfulness, your whole countenance will change, and others will be reminded that there's a God in heaven very much involved in their own lives. He intends to get us safely home. But don't wait till then to find rest in Him. Embrace a heart-at-rest kind of day.

Blessing for Child

Sometimes you need to rest. Sleep is a good thing. Taking time out to catch your breath will help you be stronger when you get back in the game. And when you take a break, remember all the things God's done for you. Smile as you think about how He protects you and gives you everything you need. Rest well in Jesus!

Whoever dwells in the
shelter of the Most High
will *rest* in the shadow
of the Almighty.

PSALM 91:1 NIV

Harvesttime

Blessing for Mom

May you sow the seeds God has given you to sow. May you reap above and beyond anything you could ever ask or think. May you know without a doubt your divine call. And may you open your arms wide and receive everything God provides along the way. Sleep well tonight.

Blessing for Child

Did you know that God has certain jobs just for you? He wants you to be kind to the hurting, and friendly to the lonely. You have some friends that He wants to get to know, and you can introduce them to Him. How exciting is that! May you always listen to what He asks you to do, because it will be so much fun to see all the wonderful things He does through you. Have a good night's sleep!

Now he who *supplies* seed to
the sower and bread for food will
also supply and *increase* your
store of seed and will enlarge the
harvest of your righteousness.
You will be *enriched* in every
way so that you can be generous
on every occasion, and through
us your generosity will result in
thanksgiving to God.

2 CORINTHIANS 9:10–11 NIV

Christ in Focus

Blessing for Mom

May God help you renew your mind and redeem your words. May you refuse thoughts that weaken you, thoughts that take your eyes off of God. May you instead embrace thoughts that are true, based on God's great love for you. May you refuse to speak about your life apart from faith. May you instead embrace faith, speak truth, and choose life every single moment of every single day. Sleep well tonight.

Blessing for Child

Don't stop looking at Jesus! It makes a big difference in what you do, what you say, and what you think. He will guide you and guard you and stay right beside you. He'll tell you what to say and how to pray. He'll even make you strong when you feel weak. Without God, everything else falls apart because He made everything! Always remember that. Good night, child of God!

We *demolish* arguments
and every pretension that
sets itself up against the
knowledge of God, and we
take captive every thought to
make it *obedient* to Christ.

2 CORINTHIANS 10:5 NIV

23

Holy Confidence

Blessing for Mom

May God release special favor over your life today! May He fill you up to overflowing and give you a fresh vision for your life. May you identify the places where the enemy has planted inferiority and insecurity and play king of the hill there! Put him under your feet and refuse to let those lies win the day. In Christ you have NO reason to feel less than or inferior. He is more than enough for you. Walk in God's truth and rest in His care. He loves you, and He will lead you in the way you should go. Have a blessed day today.

Blessing for Child

God wants you to win! Sometimes people root against you—and the devil *always* roots against you—but God is bigger than any of them. Don't let them trick you into thinking you're not good enough or smart enough or strong enough. Remind yourself daily, *I am a child of God!* He knows you best, and He says you've got everything you need to do big things for Him!

Surely, LORD, you *bless*
the righteous; you surround
them with your *favor*
as with a shield.

PSALM 5:12 NIV

24 Abounding Grace

Blessing for Mom

May you—in spite of your mistakes and missteps—see how God's love and provision more than cover you. May you—in your weakness—experience abounding grace that makes you divinely strong. Where you've experienced loss and brokenness, may you know healing, wholeness, and redemption. Your Redeemer is for you, and He is strong. Sleep well tonight.

Blessing for Child

You're going to mess up sometimes. That's normal. You're not perfect. But always know God loves you and will forgive you! Jesus is on your side, and He's strong enough for the two of you! Don't focus on your badness. Focus on God's goodness. He's enough for you. He's crazy in love with you! He'll lead you through every difficult day, and He'll take what's wrong and make it right. He's doing a great work in you. Good night, child of God.

Each time [the Lord] said, "My *grace* is all you need. My power works best in weakness." So now I am glad to *boast* about my weaknesses, so that the power of Christ can work *through* me.

2 CORINTHIANS 12:9

25

Hilarious Joy!

Blessing for Mom

May the hilarious joy of the Lord burst from your heart today! May His love sturdy your steps. May His passion fuel your steps. May His promises propel you to take faith risks. Delight in God today. He will establish you. Rejoice in Him. He will strengthen you. Trust in Him. He will not fail you. Wrap yourself up in His grace. You have what you need to abound in every good work. He's got you covered. Walk with joy and gladness today.

Blessing for Child

May God fill you so full of joy that it bursts right out of you! It'll make you strong and get you going in the right direction! He'll never let you down, and He's on your side, ready to help out when you need a hand. Always remember that, and be so thankful for all He does for you!

You will live in *joy* and *peace*. The mountains and hills will *burst* into song, and the trees of the field will *clap* their hands!

ISAIAH 55:12

An Eternal Perspective

Blessing for Mom

As you wrap up your day, may God grace you with an eternal perspective. Where there's only been disappointment, may you trust God's divine appointment and timing. Where there's been discouragement, may He inspire new courage to stand strong. Where there's been whining and griping, may you find a new song to sing and new reasons for thanksgiving. May He break through the clouds so you'll see just how blessed you are. Sleep well tonight.

Blessing for Child

God always knows what's up! He's got things under control, and you can trust Him to do things exactly when they need to be done. There's no need to whine or pout or think the sky is falling every time things don't go your way—He's got a plan, so be thankful! One day you will see His good plans play out before your very eyes. You can trust Him. Good night, my love.

You didn't choose me.
I *chose* you. I *appointed*
you to go and produce lasting
fruit, so that the Father
will *give* you whatever you
ask for, using my name.
This is my command:
Love each other.

JOHN 15:16–17

27 Hold Your Ground

Blessing for Mom

In the face of the enemy's lies, taunts, and threats, may you tighten your belt of truth, raise your shield of faith, and hold your ground. May you refuse to be bullied by your fears or pushed around by your past mistakes. May you instead look to Jesus, the Author and Finisher of your faith. May you dare to look ahead to the promised land He's offered you. You are equipped to win your fear-battle, so press in and press on today!

Blessing for Child

Sometimes it seems like there's no way you can win! The problem you're facing is too scary, or the enemy is too strong. But don't be afraid! God is like a soldier who can't be beaten, or a superhero without any weaknesses. And He's on your side! You can't lose! You are a child of God!

But the LORD is with me like a
mighty warrior;
so my persecutors will
stumble and not prevail.
They will fail and be thoroughly
disgraced; their dishonor
will *never* be forgotten.

JEREMIAH 20:11 NIV

Love in Action

Blessing for Mom

May the Lord bring fulfillment to your work, hilarity to your play, depth to your prayers, and kindness to your words. May He inspire perspective, conviction, and compassion to change the world. And tonight, may He grant blessed and sweet sleep.

Blessing for Child

May God make your work exciting, your playtime fun, your prayers deep, and your words kind. And may He show you how to live the way He wants you to live so you can change the world! You won't be able to do it without Him. But with Him, you can do whatever He puts in front of you. When you trust God more than you trust yourself, you'll be amazed at what He'll do. So tonight, may you sleep in peace.

Unless the LORD *builds* the house, the builders labor in vain. Unless the LORD *watches* over the city, the guards stand watch in vain. In vain you rise early and stay up late, toiling for food to eat—for he *grants* sleep to those he loves.

PSALM 127:1–2 NIV

29

Gritty Faith

Blessing for Mom

May the Lord himself establish you in His best purposes for you. May He strengthen you with holy conviction and gritty faith to climb every mountain He's assigned to you. May He increase your capacity to love and encourage others. And when the enemy rises up against you, may you see with your own eyes how God fights for you. You're on the winning side. Sleep well tonight.

Blessing for Child

Don't be afraid to do big things for God! He'll help you in every way you need. Climb that mountain! Plant that garden! Help that neighbor! It may be hard sometimes, but God will give you strength. God wants to do great things through you. Sleep well knowing He's on your side!

If God is *for* us, who can be against us? He who did not spare his own Son, but *gave* him up for us all— how will he not also, along with him, *graciously* give us all things? . . . No, in all these things we are more than *conquerors* through him who loved us.

ROMANS 8:31–32, 37 NIV

Remember What's True

Blessing for Mom

May God fill you with grace and power this very hour! May His love compel you to look up and remember what's true. May crystal-clear clarity replace confusion and chaos. And today, may you march onward with this truth alive in your soul: God is with you, He goes before you, and He has your back. You are MORE than your circumstances. You are someone whom God loves and empowers to live valiantly. Blessings on your day today.

Blessing for Child

Be strong! Be powerful! God loves you, and don't ever forget it! When you feel confused, ask God to make things clear to you. He's generous with His wisdom. When you feel weak, ask Him for strength. When you feel afraid, ask Him to remind you how much He loves you. He's got you. And remember what's true: God will never leave you. He is always holding on to you. God bless your day!

A final word: Be *strong* in the Lord and in his *mighty* power.

EPHESIANS 6:10

Entrust Your Cares

Blessing for Mom

May you open your hands and entrust your cares to God. Right this minute. Know this: Jesus knows your name, has your address, and loves who you are. He will get you where you need to go. He will reach out to the ones you love. He will validate and vindicate you at the proper time. May you see and believe that you're safest when you're at His feet, trusting Him to do what you cannot do for yourself. May your soul find rest in Him today.

Blessing for Child

When there are tough things on your mind—things you can't decide about or things you're scared of, or stuff you don't want to do that you have to do anyway—you can always go to God. You can give Him your questions and your fears, and He'll take them and help you figure out what to do. You're always safe when you're trusting God for help! Relax, He's got you covered.

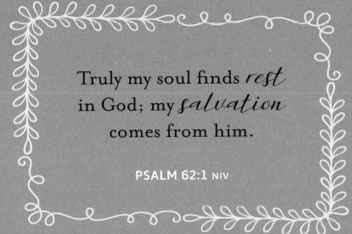

Truly my soul finds *rest*
in God; my *salvation*
comes from him.

PSALM 62:1 NIV

Equipped for Victory

Blessing for Mom

(Speak this over yourself): I am loved, called, and chosen. I am rich in every way and generous on every occasion. I'm anointed, appointed, equipped, and enabled by the power of God that works mightily within me! No weapon formed against me will prosper, and no enemy scheme against me will succeed. I live, breathe, and serve powerfully under the shelter of the Most High God. Amen.

Blessing for Child

God loves you, and He picked you to be in His family! How great is that? Sometimes it looks like other people have more money or are smarter or stronger. But you can't lose when you're on God's team! Even the strongest or meanest people in the world are no match for Him. Ask God to give you the kind of confidence that cannot be shaken. He'll do that for you.

"No weapon forged against you will prevail, and you will *refute* every tongue that accuses you. This is the *heritage* of the servants of the LORD, and this is their vindication from me," declares the LORD.

ISAIAH 54:17 NIV

33 God Is Working for You

Blessing for Mom

As the day draws to a close, may you embrace God's grace, trusting He'll fill every gap. Instead of being unsettled by your imperfections, may you be undone by Jesus' perfect love for you. Instead of fretting over your missteps, rejoice that He never left your side today. Scoop this day into your hand and lift it up as an offering to the One who moves mountains and ministers miracles with every little handful we give Him. He's a miracle-working God, and He loves you.

Blessing for Child

Think about your day. Did you do anything bad? Ask God to forgive you! He always will, and He'll never leave your side. Hold your hand out to God and give Him your day, the good and the bad. He is big enough to move a mountain, so He can easily take your day and turn it into something good.

We know that God causes everything to *work together* for the good of those who love God and are *called* according to his purpose for them.

ROMANS 8:28

He Loves and He Restores

Blessing for Mom

May God himself recover and restore what the enemy has stolen. May He heal family rifts, renew tired relationships, and revive weary faith. May He lift you up and make you strong. May He give you wisdom in boundaries and humility in love. May He show you what's yours and give you grace to release what isn't. And may you know beyond a shadow of a doubt that nothing and no one can separate you from God's love. Walk in humble, hopeful faith today.

Blessing for Child

When bad things happen, it may feel like you lost something big. Maybe you got into an argument with someone and feel like you lost a friend. Or you got sick on the weekend and feel like you missed out on a day of fun. Whatever you think you've lost, trust that God is strong enough to get it back. And know that nothing you ever do can separate you from God!

I'm *absolutely convinced* that nothing—nothing living or dead, angelic or demonic, today or tomorrow, high or low, thinkable or unthinkable— absolutely *nothing* can get between us and God's love because of the way that Jesus our Master has *embraced* us.

ROMANS 8:38–39 MSG

His Presence and Promises

Blessing for Mom

May Jesus' presence be especially tangible to you today. May the reality of His love sink deep into your bones. May His faithfulness be your anchor, His promises be your protection, and His presence be your joy. God is faithful; it's impossible for Him to fail you. He's made promises to you that He intends to keep. And His presence changes EVERYTHING. Enjoy and embrace the access God has offered you today.

Blessing for Child

I hope you can feel God's presence today. He smiles when He thinks of you! When you dare to believe that He really, really loves you, you'll dare to trust Him with the things that stress you out. He's right by your side. He's there and will always keep you safe. Talk to Him! Ask Him to give you joy and peace, and trust that He is always good.

I bow before your holy Temple as I *worship*. I praise your name for your *unfailing* love and faithfulness; for your promises are backed by all the *honor* of your name.

PSALM 138:2

36

Snuggled by God

Blessing for Mom

As you get ready to crawl into bed tonight, may you hand Jesus your worries and grab hold of His peace and perspective. May you lay down your judgments and hold close His fresh mercies. As you crawl under the covers, remember you're not under your circumstances; you are under the shadow of His wing. Take hold of what you possess in Him. Sleep well.

Blessing for Child

As you get ready to go to sleep, give Jesus all the things you're scared about. Let Him trade you: He'll take your fear and give you His courage. Don't think about all the stuff you've done wrong. Think about how much Jesus loves you and forgives you. Picture yourself as a baby bird and Jesus as a mother bird with His wing protecting you and keeping you warm. Snuggle up close to Him as you go to sleep.

He will *cover* you with his feathers. He will *shelter* you with his wings. His *faithful* promises are your armor and protection.

PSALM 91:4

37 See Yourself through His Eyes

Blessing for Mom

May God open your Spirit-eyes to see your life, your worth, and your destiny from His point of view. He's doing a beautiful work in you! May you open wide your arms and receive His abundant love, His powerful promises, and His moment-by-moment faithfulness. He will not fail you! May you live as one who is spoken for, provided for, and deeply loved. Because you are. Have a great day!

Blessing for Child

Stretch out your arms as wide as you can. Did you know that God loves you even more than that? You are SO precious to Him! He's making you into something incredible as you grow bigger and stronger every day. He'll never leave your side. You're loved more than you could ever understand. Believe it! Have a great day!

Here is my servant, whom I uphold, my *chosen* one in whom I delight; I will put my Spirit on him, and he will bring *justice* to the nations.

ISAIAH 42:1 NIV

38

God Is for You

Blessing for Mom

May God remove every hindrance that keeps you from knowing His love in a way that changes you. May He change every circumstance that sends a lying message to you. May He highlight every trial He's using to train you to be a warrior. And may He remind you that all of heaven is on your side. You are very close to His heart. Sleep well.

Blessing for Child

Just as the clouds sometimes block the sun, things in life can sometimes block your view of God. Maybe you've had a bad day, or you did something wrong, or somebody said mean things to you. Just because you can't see the sun doesn't mean it isn't shining. It's the same with God. Just because you can't feel Him doesn't mean He isn't there. God doesn't disappear when life is hard. He's right by your side. He will turn this around. And He's turning you into a mighty warrior in the meantime! You can trust Him. Rest in His care tonight, my precious child.

Even before he *made* the world, God loved us and *chose* us in Christ to be *holy* and without fault in his eyes.

EPHESIANS 1:4

Coming against the Enemy

Blessing for Mom

May God give you faith to put fear under your feet. May you know that for every way the enemy comes against you, the Lord has a promise to bless you and to help you stand strong. May you fix your eyes on Jesus and set your heart on His Word. Know this: When the enemy comes in like a flood, the Lord will raise up a standard against him! Trust in God and sleep in peace tonight.

Blessing for Child

Sometimes you will face enemies—everybody does. Maybe there's a teacher who doesn't like you, or a kid on the playground who bullies you. But that doesn't mean you should be afraid. God is on your side, ready to fight for you! He will make you strong. He'll show you what to do. Trust in God and have a good night's sleep.

So shall they *fear* the name
of the LORD from the west, and
His *glory* from the rising
of the sun; when the enemy
comes in like a flood, the
Spirit of the LORD will *lift*
up a standard against him.

ISAIAH 59:19 NKJV

God Is in Control

Blessing for Mom

May you be assured on a whole new level of how much God loves you and that He's constantly working on your behalf. May you feel a fresh surge of confidence amidst your circumstances because you know that God is ultimately in control, and nothing escapes His notice. He only allows battles you can win, and in every one there are treasures and spoils with your name on them. Live bravely today!

Blessing for Child

Did you know that God is in charge of EVERYTHING? He knows what you're doing right now, what you're scared of, what you're going to do later, and how it will all work out. And what's more, He's got big plans for you to win! You can stand tall, knowing God has everything already worked out. Be brave with God on your side!

Therefore, my dear brothers
and sisters, *stand firm*.
Let nothing move you. Always
give yourselves *fully* to the
work of the Lord, because
you know that your labor in
the Lord is *not in vain*.

1 CORINTHIANS 15:58 NIV

Fearing God, Not Man

Blessing for Mom

May you be content to know that you cannot be all things to all people; you live to serve an audience of One. May you love people but keep your hope in God. May you be willing to take risks with people, but may your sole trust be in God. May the power you once gave to others rest solely on God because He defines, He saves, He provides, and He has the power to transform. Sleep well.

Blessing for Child

Sometimes you want to say something but you're scared of what other people will think. Or maybe you know something is wrong, but you want to do it anyway to make people like you or make them laugh. Though it feels good when people like you, true friends will always want you to do the right thing. Besides, it's much more important to do what God wants you to do. Always trust in Him instead of in what other people think. And sleep well tonight. God is for you!

Fearing people is a
dangerous trap,
but *trusting* the
LORD means safety.

PROVERBS 29:25

Seeing beyond Obstacles

Blessing for Mom

May God open your eyes to see beyond the obstacles and through the storm so you can envision His next place of promise for you. May your doubts, worries, and fears take a back seat to faith, hope, and love. In fact, may others look up from their own storm because of how you trust God in yours. You are mighty in battle because God is mighty in you! Don't give up hope. Don't coddle your fears. Cling to the promises of God and walk forward in faith. Have a brave and courageous day.

Blessing for Child

Sometimes bad things happen even to people who love God. Be ready for that, but don't be scared. Instead, remember that God promises He will always be with you and that good things are coming. He loves you, and you can count on that, even on very bad days. Be brave today!

When you ask, you must
believe and not doubt,
because the one who doubts is
like a *wave* of the sea, blown
and tossed by the *wind*.

JAMES 1:6 NIV

The Rock

Blessing for Mom

May God's love and truth bring clarity and purpose to your life. May His strength steady your steps. May His compassion open your eyes, and may His conviction make your heart beat strong. May His kingdom come and His will be done in and through you. And tonight, sleep well.

Blessing for Child

May God help you go exactly where you're supposed to go and know exactly what you should do. With Jesus in your heart, you have all of heaven on your side. He's teaching you how to walk with Him. Listen for His voice and do what He says. He'll make you like a deer with steady feet that never trip on the rocks. Have a great night of sleep!

As for God, his way is *perfect*:
The LORD's word is flawless;
he *shields* all who take
refuge in him. For who is God
besides the LORD? And who
is the Rock except our God?
It is God who arms me with
strength and keeps my way
secure. He makes my feet like
the feet of a deer; he causes me
to *stand* on the heights.

2 SAMUEL 22:31–34 NIV

Grateful Living

Blessing for Mom

May you wrap your arms around the ones you love, look them in the eyes, and tell them how much you treasure them. May you look around and take notice of all the blessings you'd miss if they went away tomorrow. When you're tempted to indulge in melancholy or discontentment, may you instead jump up, raise your hands, and thank God for His daily and divine intervention in your life. May your humble gratitude give you keen spiritual insight. Rest well tonight.

Blessing for Child

Tell the people you love how much you love them! Be so thankful for all God has given you: the people in your life, your house, your food, the birds and trees and beautiful skies. Don't be grumpy. Instead, jump up and bounce around, and be grateful to God for everything you have. You are more blessed than you know! And sleep well tonight.

May the God of your father
help you; may the Almighty
bless you with the blessings
of the heavens above, and
blessings of the watery depths
below, and blessings of the
breasts and womb. May my
fatherly *blessings* on you
surpass the blessings of my
ancestors, reaching to the
heights of the eternal hills.
May these blessings rest on
the head of Joseph, who is a
prince among his brothers.

GENESIS 49:25–26

Give Him Access to You

Blessing for Mom

May you give God full access to your story. May you allow Him to correct and redirect, heal and deal, refine and define, whenever it suits Him. He loves you most and knows what's best for you at every given moment. He will lead you in the way you should go. May you remember that you're part of a great story God is writing in the world. May you trust the Lord's work in your life so He can use you in ways beyond your wildest dreams. Lean in and trust Him. He's got you.

Blessing for Child

Always talk to God. Tell Him how you feel, the good and the bad. He knows you perfectly, so nothing you say will surprise Him. And the more you talk to Him, the better you'll know Him and how much He loves you. Cuddle up with Him and tell Him all about yourself. He's holding you tight!

LORD my God, I *called* to you for help, and you *healed* me.

PSALM 30:2 NIV

Momentary Troubles

Blessing for Mom

May the Lord himself give you a fresh perspective on your life. May you begin to see your troubles—tough as they are—as momentary. In fact, may you wrap your arms around the promise that those very troubles are achieving for you an eternal glory that far outweighs them all. Jesus is deeply invested in your journey and intends to get you safely home. May He give you a glimpse of glory, a peek into the eternal significance of your life. You matter deeply to Him. May your spirit be renewed in His presence today.

Blessing for Child

Did something make you sad today? I'm so sorry you are hurting, and so is God. But someday all sadness will disappear. Nothing bad lasts forever, but good things do, because God is forever, and He's the creator of all good things. So for now, we patiently trust God to care for us, and we keep praying and believing. Someday we'll get to live with Him in heaven in a perfect world. May you live loved, even when life is hard. Heaven is going to be wonderful. Jesus cares about your life, and He's got amazing plans for you.

For our light and momentary troubles are *achieving* for us an *eternal* glory that far outweighs them all.

2 CORINTHIANS 4:17 NIV

From Fearful to Joyful

Blessing for Mom

May God surround you with His tender mercies and encompass you with a fresh revelation of His love. May He keep you hidden away from toxic people and strengthen your healthy relationships. May He bless you with a new friend who sees what He sees in you. And may you rest tonight knowing He'll be there to greet you in the morning. Sleep deeply, sleep well.

Blessing for Child

May you fill up your life with good people who love God and encourage you to know Him better. May God give you a brand-new friend who knows how special you are. May He remind you throughout the day how blessed you are. When you count the good things in your life, you will feel glad instead of sad. In the morning God will greet you with a big smile. So sleep well tonight!

May all who fear you *find* in me a cause for *joy*, for I have put my *hope* in your word.

PSALM 119:74

48 Freedom in Christ

Blessing for Mom

It is *for* freedom that Christ has set you free. May you refuse to be subject to any yoke of slavery—slavery to sin, fear, legalism, or striving. May you rest in the knowledge that Jesus paid it all so that you could walk free and whole. May you boldly live the abundant, fruitful life He had in mind from the beginning. You are everything to Him.

Blessing for Child

Dear child, may you know that it's not your job to make everybody happy or to make everybody like you. You're already loved! Jesus came to earth because He loved you. He died for your sins. He rose from the grave to set you free. Now you are free to grow into the person He made you to be! May you really believe—with all of your heart—that you have nothing to prove because Jesus is enough for you. He'll teach you how to live a holy, honorable life that pleases Him.

It is for *freedom* that
Christ has set us free.
Stand firm, then, and do
not let yourselves be burdened
again by a *yoke* of slavery.

GALATIANS 5:1 NIV

A Better Tomorrow

Blessing for Mom

May you find a moment of peace and quiet tonight to thank God for all that is right in your world. May you have the presence of mind to release your cares and worries to Him. May you have the gritty faith to grab a firmer grip on His promises to you. And may you wake up in the morning knowing that you've gained ground even during your sleeping hours because God is always moving on your behalf. As you entrust your whole self to Him today, He'll get you where you need to go tomorrow. Sleep well tonight.

Blessing for Child

My precious child, let's pause and count our blessings tonight. May you talk to God about all the great stuff He's doing in your life. Then, take all the things that make you scared and hand them over to Him. He promises to take care of you! Did you know that God is working to help you with your problems even when you're asleep? You're always on the right path when you stick with Him! Good night, and know that God loves you.

Let us hold *unswervingly* to the hope we profess, for he who promised is *faithful*.

HEBREWS 10:23 NIV

A Fruitful Life

Blessing for Mom

May you walk with a new confidence that in Christ you are prized, loved, accepted, called, equipped, and sent out to change the world. You lack no good thing! And tonight, may you rest in His shadow. He's got you.

Blessing for Child

May you grow up big and strong, knowing that God thinks the world of you! There's nothing He wouldn't do for you, so you can go out and achieve amazing things for Him. So tonight, curl up under His arm and sleep well.

But the godly will *flourish* like palm trees and grow strong like the cedars of Lebanon. For they are transplanted to the LORD's own *house*. They flourish in the courts of our God. Even in old age they will still *produce* fruit; they will remain vital and green.

PSALM 92:12–14

Unshakable

Blessing for Mom

In this day of uncertainty, may God give you a faith that cannot be shaken. When all is in chaos, may you have divine clarity to see God's highest will and divine movement all around you. May you know peace that passes understanding and pass it on to others. Stand strong, my friend! You possess all in Him. Walk forward unafraid.

Blessing for Child

Sometimes the world is a messed-up place filled with scary things, and it feels like no one knows what's going on or what will happen next. Through it all, may God give you great faith in Him. He is in charge of everything! He can give you an amazing peace that helps you stand strong. Don't be afraid!

Then Job replied to the LORD:
"I know that you can do
anything, and no one can
stop you. You asked, 'Who is
this that questions my *wisdom*
with such ignorance?' It is I—
and I was talking about things
I knew nothing about, things
far too *wonderful* for me."

JOB 42:1–3

52

Have Fun

Blessing for Mom

May you count your blessings today out loud, one by one, in a louder voice than you'd usually use (it's hilariously fun that way). May you remember a time you belly-laughed with a friend, and smile at the thought of it. May you put on a song that makes you dance and shout and thank God for the freedoms you enjoy. And may you stretch your arms out in faith, full of expectancy that your future days will be brighter than your past. God is on the throne, working on your behalf, and He's always good.

Blessing for Child

Count your blessings! Do you know what that means? It means to thank God for all the things He has given you—good friends, belly laughs, great music, and letting you live in a free country. And don't just count them, shout them! Thank God in a loud voice for all He's done. God is the King of everything, and you can expect other blessings to come your way too. He cares about what happens to you, and He is always good!

Give *thanks* to the LORD, for he is good! His faithful love endures *forever*.

PSALM 107:1

53

Your New Future

Blessing for Mom

May God lift you up and heal and restore you fully. May you see glimpses of His glory everywhere you turn. May He show you wonders of His love that overwhelm you and make your knees weak. May He put a new song in your heart and a new dream in your spirit. May you walk forward unafraid and full of faith that your future will be far greater than your past.

Blessing for Child

I know life hurts sometimes, but did you know that God can heal you? You may be hurting on the outside—a skinned knee, a broken bone, or even worse. Or you may be hurting on the inside, if you're lonely or scared or someone was mean to you. But no matter how you're hurting, God can turn things around and make things better than ever! He is always up to something good. You can trust Him.

The LORD says, "I will *give* you back what you lost to the swarming locusts, the hopping locusts, the stripping locusts, and the cutting locusts. It was I who sent this great destroying army against you. Once again you will have all the food you want, and you will *praise* the LORD your God, who does these *miracles* for you. Never again will my people be disgraced."

JOEL 2:25–26

Trust Him Fully

Blessing for Mom

May you dare to trust in the Lord with your whole heart and not lean on your own understanding. May you look up and acknowledge Him with every step you take, knowing He'll get you where you need to go. May you put your hope in Him and not in the approval of other people. God will never disappoint. He loves you more than you can comprehend. Trust Him, and soon your eyes will see how good He is. Blessings on your day today!

Blessings for Child

Sometimes things just don't go the way we want them to, or we're just in a bad mood. But look up! Tell yourself to cheer up. Everything's going to be okay. God will get you where you need to go. Put your hope in Him and don't worry about what anyone else says! He loves you so much. May you open your eyes and see how good God really is. Have a great day!

Why, my soul, are you downcast? Why so disturbed within me? Put your *hope* in God, for I will yet praise him, my *Savior* and my *God*.

PSALM 42:5 NIV

Pray Tenaciously

Blessing for Mom

May you look around and notice all the answers to prayer you enjoy because of what you prayed some time ago. May the breakthroughs you've experienced and the open doors you've walked through compel you to pray with more fervency, specificity, and tenacity. God loves your faith. He loves it when you pray. He's very protective of you and won't give you something that's not good for you. He makes you wait because He's making you ready. Keep praying. God is moving, even when you can't see it. One day, your faith will become sight.

Blessing for Child

Can you remember some of the things you've prayed for and how God has taken care of you? God has been good to you in so many ways! He loves it when you pray, and He wants to give you great things. Keep praying! God is always doing wonderful things, and He wants you to talk to Him. One day you'll see so many more things He's done.

Rejoice *always*, pray *continually*, give thanks in all circumstances; for this is God's *will* for you in Christ Jesus.

1 THESSALONIANS 5:16–18 NIV

A Mighty Move of God

Blessing for Mom

May you have a strong sense of the impossible things God wants to do in, through, and around you. May God's dream for you swallow up your unbelief! May you have faith enough to put out your buckets and prepare for rain. God moves on faith. May He move mightily because of yours. And tonight, enjoy restful, faith-filled sleep. God is mighty to save.

Blessing for Child

May you grow to know and believe that God wants to do big things in your life! I know it's hard to see sometimes, but that's why your faith matters so much. May you trust that God is up to something good, and He wants you to be a part of it. Have a great night of sleep as you dream about tomorrow.

Forget the former things; do not *dwell* on the past. See, I am doing a *new* thing! Now it springs up; do you not perceive it? I am making a *way* in the wilderness and streams in the wasteland.

ISAIAH 43:18–19 NIV

Abundantly Blessed

Blessing for Mom

May abundant grace and profound peace be multiplied to you in every way. May countless blessings chase and overtake you, and may you notice when they do. May God heal your heart, soul, mind, and body, and may you approach life with eternity in mind. May you know the wholeness God always intended for you, and may your faith be renewed. Have a great day. Look for Him expectantly today!

Blessing for Child

Have you ever been outside when rain suddenly starts to fall so hard it feels like you're standing under a waterfall? That's the way God wants to bless you! May you throw your head back, open your hands, believe it, and receive it! God wants to rain good things down on your head until you're completely soaked, head to toe, in peace and joy and love! That's what heaven will look like, but God wants you to experience some of that even now. Have a great day!

Curses chase *sinners*, while *blessings* chase the righteous!

PROVERBS 13:21 TLB

Secure in Christ

Blessing for Mom

May you understand on a greater level your secure standing in Christ. May you approach Him with fresh boldness and faith, assured of His glad welcome. May your prayers move heaven and earth, and may you remember that everywhere you place your feet, God's kingdom comes to earth.

Blessing for Child

Did you know that if you have Jesus in your heart, He'll never leave you? That's a promise! So be brave and know that He can't wait to talk to you. Ask Him for big things. Believe that He wants to do great things in and all around you! When you talk to God, He listens, and wherever you go, He's right there by your side. May you learn how to pray big prayers to your big God. He loves to hear from you.

Through *followers* of Jesus
like yourselves gathered in
churches, this extraordinary
plan of God is becoming
known and talked about even
among the angels! All this
is proceeding along lines
planned all along by God
and then executed in Christ
Jesus. When we *trust* in him,
we're *free* to say whatever
needs to be said, bold to go
wherever we need to go.

EPHESIANS 3:10–12 MSG

You're an Heir

Blessing for Mom

May you walk and talk and pray and live in a manner worthy of your royal status in Christ Jesus. May you believe with your whole heart that you are positioned right where you are for such a time as this. May God increase your influence, anoint your words, and appoint your everyday moments. You are an ambassador for the Most High God. Live like it is true, because it is. Blessings upon you this day!

Blessing for Child

Jesus is the King. And when you accept Jesus into your heart, you become part of His family. That means you are royalty! Think about that. May you live your life knowing this is true. You are part of the ultimate royal family! May you feel this truth from the top of your head to the tip of your toes. May your secure place in the kingdom family change everything you say and do. You are a child of the God who rules the entire universe! Be blessed today.

But to all who *believed* him and accepted him, he gave the right to become *children* of God.

JOHN 1:12

Good Gifts

Blessing for Mom

May you slow down long enough tomorrow to enjoy the sacredness of the present moment. May God give you plenty of sacred pauses to reflect on His intimate and powerful love for you. May you enjoy lots of face-to-face encounters with those you love. May God open your eyes and use you to lift up those bent beneath heavy loads. May *you* receive the gifts He so lovingly wants to give. And tonight, may you enjoy deep, refreshing sleep. Tomorrow's a new day.

Blessing for Child

Sometimes life moves too quickly. We forget to slow down and think about all the great things we get to do and see. May you love the time you spend with your family and your friends. And may you notice people around you who aren't having a good time—sick people or sad people—and do your best to help them or cheer them up. God has given you so much! Have a great night's sleep and dream about all the fun you'll have tomorrow!

If you then, being evil, know how to give *good* gifts to your children, how much more will your heavenly Father *give* the Holy Spirit to those who *ask* Him!

LUKE 11:13 NKJV

61

A Peace Offering

Blessing for Mom

May God give you kindness and grace for those who step on your toes. May He give you holy and humble confidence in the presence of those who misunderstand you. May He give you love and forgiveness for those who hurt you and grace for those who miss you completely. And may His love spill over you till you know that you are everything to Him. Sleep well tonight. Walk confidently tomorrow.

Blessing for Child

May God help you forgive those who hurt you, even if they don't understand what they've done, because that's what Jesus has done for you! And may you remember that sometimes you hurt people too! We all say things we shouldn't or treat people in ways that we wouldn't want to be treated. That's why we're so blessed to have a Savior who taught us how to love, live, and forgive every single day. He loves you so much, and you are so valuable to him. Have a good night's sleep and a great day tomorrow!

Since God chose you to be the *holy* people he loves, you must clothe yourselves with tenderhearted mercy, kindness, humility, gentleness, and patience. Make allowance for each other's faults, and forgive anyone who offends you. Remember, the Lord *forgave* you, so you must forgive others. Above all, clothe yourselves with *love*, which binds us all together in perfect *harmony*. And let the peace that comes from Christ rule in your hearts. For as members of one body you are called to live in *peace*. And always be thankful.

COLOSSIANS 3:12–15

A Playful Moment

Blessing for Mom

May you face today with a smile and with hopeful expectancy. May God surprise you with a song that speaks to your heart. May you enjoy a sudden playful moment and enter in with your whole heart. And may you notice that every good gift in your life comes from above. In every season, He gives good gifts to His children. A blessed and wonderful day to you this day!

Blessing for Child

Smile and be ready for great things today! I hope God fills you with fun surprises that you didn't see coming. Remember: All the good things you have come from God. He loves to give presents to His children! And He loves it when you're just as generous to others. God wants to bless you, and bless the world through you. Have a wonderful day!

Every good and perfect gift
is from *above*, coming
down from the Father of the
heavenly lights, who does not
change like shifting shadows.

JAMES 1:17 NIV

63

A Thankful Heart

Blessing for Mom

May you set aside your fears, worries, and frustrations, and pull close the ones you love. May you notice and give thanks for all that is right in your world. May the Lord become especially real to you in the coming days. And may you grow in your capacity to thank Him and trust Him in every single circumstance. Enjoy sweet rest tonight.

Blessing for Child

Dear child, may you grow to know that the best medicine for fear and worry is love and thankfulness. When you remember God's amazing love for you, your heart won't be afraid. And when you begin to thank Him for all He's done, you'll remember that He is good. We all get scared sometimes, but God wants you to throw away your fears and trust Him. May Jesus feel so close, it's like you're cuddling right up against Him. He is here with you now, and He'll never let you go. Sleep well!

Don't worry about anything; instead, *pray* about everything. Tell God what you need, and *thank* him for all he has done. Then you will experience God's *peace*, which exceeds anything we can understand. His peace will *guard* your hearts and minds as you live in Christ Jesus.

PHILIPPIANS 4:6–7

64 Keep Perspective

Blessing for Mom

May you ponder what God is saying to you in this place of not-yets and what-ifs. Do you hear His whisper to be still and to trust Him? May you dream big dreams in the face of your fears. May you courageously hold your ground when you'd rather run and hide. And may you entrust your heart's desires to a God who is very much involved, very much in control, and very much invested in your life. Remember who you are. Remember Whose you are. Keep perspective. Lay hold of faith. Take the next step.

Blessings for Child

Did you know that God sees the future? He knows what will happen to you tomorrow, and the next day, and the next. And He loves you so much and is watching over you. So you can trust Him with your dreams about the future because He wants what's best for you. Don't ever forget that!

From the ends of the earth I *call* to you, I call as my heart grows faint; *lead* me to the rock that is higher than I.

PSALM 61:2 NIV

Your Story and God's

Blessing for Mom

May you grow to love and accept the *you* God is making you to be. May you walk in a new level of grace and gratitude that gives you peace and leaves others encouraged. May you be more apt to look forward with hope than you are to look back with regret. May your heart spill over with joy at the very thought of the story God is writing with your life. Sleep deeply tonight.

Blessing for Child

May you do your very best not to look at other kids and want to trade places with them. God made you special and loves you just the way you are. Jump up and down in excitement about the way God made you, because that's exactly how God feels. He's so excited about you, and He can't wait to watch what you'll do with your life. Have a great night's sleep!

Always be full of *joy* in
the Lord. I say it again—
rejoice! Let everyone see
that you are considerate in
all you do. Remember, the
Lord is *coming soon*.

PHILIPPIANS 4:4–5

Keep Walking

Blessing for Mom

May you dare to keep walking even though quitting feels like the easier thing to do. May you dare to look up even though the weight of your burden compels you to look down. May you dare to dream about the future even though the enemy would love for your past to have the last say. Keep walking, keep looking up, and keep daring to dream. Jesus invites you forward. Embrace joy today, and don't give up!

Blessing for Child

Even though we live in a world where people like to quit, may you be someone who knows how to hang in there until God says you're done. It's easy to quit when things get tough. But don't do it! It's so good for you to push through and work hard. When you refuse to quit, you grow bigger and stronger and learn how to trust in God when it's hard. God will make you stronger than you ever dreamed possible. Keep moving on, dreaming big dreams, and never give up!

I pray that out of his *glorious* riches he may strengthen you with power through his Spirit in your *inner being*.

EPHESIANS 3:16 NIV

Through God's Eyes

Blessing for Mom

May God give you His perspective on the things that frustrate you. May your heart of compassion grow for those who suffer in unimaginable ways. May you pray as passionately for them as you do for yourself. May God protect you from a small, selfish mindset. May He fill you up with thanksgiving and joy for the freedoms you enjoy! May He renew your resolve to be a grateful, humble soul. And may He use you tomorrow in ways that surprise and bless you. Sleep well tonight.

Blessing for Child

I'm sorry you had a bad day. Everybody has days that make us sad or angry. But bad days can teach us how to care for other people who are suffering in even bigger ways than we are! May you learn how to pray for those people, and may God protect you from only thinking about yourself. I pray that you are so thankful for all the things you have and all you get to do. It's so good to be humble and grateful. Tomorrow is a new day—may God fill it with fun surprises. Have a great night's sleep.

Be joyful in *hope*, patient in *affliction*, faithful in *prayer*.

ROMANS 12:12 NIV

Fully Restored

Blessing for Mom

May God himself restore to you something you lost and never thought you'd get back again. May He heal a soul wound you thought you'd never get over. May He pour out an abundance of joy and hope that makes you celebrate before the answer comes. And may a thriving, rich faith mark your life in every way. You have access to the Most High God. May you live accordingly. Rest easy tonight!

Blessing for Child

I'm so sorry you're hurting tonight! May God give you back everything you lost and more. I pray He gives you so much joy and excitement for the future that you jump up and down for joy. May your huge faith in Him show up in everything you do because God is right there with you, ready to hear your prayers. Sleep well, child of God!

The thief comes only to
steal and kill and destroy;
I have come that they
may have *life*, and
have it to the *full*.

JOHN 10:10 NIV

Listen for Him

Blessing for Mom

May you be so sensitive to God's voice that you rest when He says to rest and to run when He says to run. He knows what's best for you, and He'll get you where you need to go. When it comes to your pace and your choices, people will always have their opinions about you, but God offers His power to you. He's the one who knows your frame, your steps, and your story. Trust Him and do what He says. Though there are giants in the land, you have God on your side. Be courageous. He's got you.

Blessing for Child

Listen to God and don't worry about what anybody else says! May you go when He says go and stop when He says stop. He knows you inside and out, and He can help you get exactly where you need to be. Yes, there are big, scary giants out there—bullies of all shapes and sizes—but bullies aren't really that brave, and you've got God on your team. Be courageous! You're in His hands.

Trust GOD from the bottom of your *heart*; don't try to figure out everything on your own. *Listen* for GOD's voice in everything you do, everywhere you go; he's the one who will keep you on *track*.

PROVERBS 3:5–6 MSG

While You Rest

Blessing for Mom

May God work mightily tonight while you rest. May He move mountains on your behalf. May He part the waters so you can pass through to your next place of promise. May you grow in the knowledge of God's love and become a flow-through account of His blessings to a world in need. Sleep well tonight.

Blessings for Child

God can do amazing things. Do you remember when He made the sun stand still so the Israelites could win a battle? Or when He separated the Red Sea so His people could get away from the Egyptians? He can still do all those things today. While you sleep, may God do big things so that your faith grows and you truly believe that you have nothing to fear. You have every reason to be confident in God. May He use you to bless the people around you too. Have a great night's sleep!

The LORD is *gracious*
and *righteous*; our God
is full of compassion. The
LORD *protects* the unwary;
when I was brought low, he
saved me. Return to your
rest, my soul, for the LORD
has been *good* to you.

PSALM 116:5–7 NIV

Purpose in Every Step

Blessing for Mom

May God establish you in His highest and best purposes for you. May He point out your time-wasters and life-drainers, and may you have the grit to walk away from them. May His passion become your passion so that your life reflects His abundant-life plan for you. And tonight, may your sleep heal and restore you in every way. You're treasured and blessed.

Blessing for Child

God is taking care of you, but He also wants you to work hard! May He teach you how to do your homework and exercise right and listen to your coaches and try your very best in everything you do. And may you learn not to waste your time on things that don't matter, things that won't bring joy to you or anybody else. And tonight, may you get the sleep you need to be fresh and ready to go tomorrow! You are so precious to God and to me.

Don't you realize that in a race everyone runs, but only *one* person gets the prize? So run to win! All athletes are *disciplined* in their training. They do it to win a prize that will fade away, but we do it for an *eternal* prize. So I run with purpose in every step. I am not just shadowboxing. I discipline my body like an athlete, *training* it to do what it should. Otherwise, I fear that after preaching to others I myself might be disqualified.

1 CORINTHIANS 9:24–27

72
Abundant Living and Giving

Blessing for Mom

May God prosper you in every way. May you be emotionally strong and stable, spiritually deep and thriving, financially free and generous, socially blessed and a blessing, and physically fit and healthy. May God fill in every gap, heal every wound, and restore everything stolen. May you live abundantly in every way. And may you sleep well tonight.

Blessing for Child

I hope and pray that you grow to be strong and smart and healthy. May you also have wonderful friends, and always follow God in everything you do. You are such a joy to me. I love that you know the difference between right and wrong and that you do your very best to tell the truth. Keep it up! I'm rooting for you! And even more important, God is with you and for you!

Dear friend, I pray that you may *enjoy* good health and that all may go well with you, even as your *soul* is getting along well. It gave me great *joy* when some believers came and testified about your faithfulness to the *truth*, telling how you continue to walk in it.

3 JOHN 1:2–3 NIV

73 Raise Your Shield

Blessing for Mom

May you raise your shield of faith, draw a line in the sand, and tell that enemy of your soul, "No more! You will steal from me no longer!" Refuse to be bullied by your fears. Don't put up with the enemy's taunts and threats. Put him under your feet, where he belongs. Remember the authority you have in Christ. Pray God's Word with all the passion in your soul. Raise your shield and lift your voice. God has made you an overcomer!

Blessing for Child

Be brave in the face of the devil! Don't be scared—God has given you what you need. You have a shield of faith, so you can tell your enemy, "No! I'm not listening." And you have the Bible, which is a sword you can use to fight back. Memorize a verse. Say it and pray it until you know it really well. Don't pay any attention to the mean things the devil says about you—remind yourself, *I am a child of God, and I have everything I need in Him!* Jesus loves you, and you can win!

Stand firm . . . [and] take up the *shield of faith*, with which you can extinguish all the flaming arrows of the evil one.

EPHESIANS 6:14, 16 NIV

Say Yes

Blessing for Mom

May Jesus bring clarity to His future plans for you. May you suddenly be assured on a much greater level of His deep love for you and of His intimate attention to detail. As He bids you to come, may you let go of what feels safe to lay hold of the new place He has for you. He's doing a new thing; don't hang on to the old just because you know it so well—don't miss out on the invitation. Take the next faith step in front of you, and have a blessed and beautiful day!

Blessing for Child

My dear child, I love you so much, and God loves you even more. He is so excited about you, and He has big plans for your future. Will you dare to say yes to Him? Open your hands and say, "I am yours, Lord! I want to serve you. I will follow you forever." He will faithfully teach you to be brave. He'll lead you to new places, and He'll use you to change the world. Don't miss out on all the great things God has for you. Have a wonderful, beautiful day!

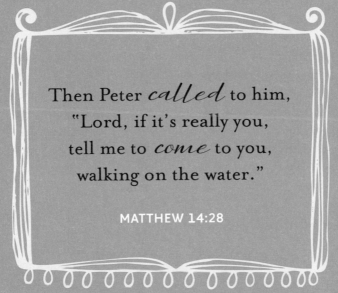

Then Peter *called* to him,
"Lord, if it's really you,
tell me to *come* to you,
walking on the water."

MATTHEW 14:28

You're a Masterpiece

Blessing for Mom

As you walk intimately with Jesus, may faith feel as natural to you as breathing in and breathing out. Pause throughout the day to look at the sky, to notice a child, or to help someone in need, and remember that you belong to Creator God. He made you for a purpose and placed you on this earth for such a time as this. Breathe in His promises, breathe out His Word, and remember His goodness. You are His masterpiece. Walk with joyful, humble, bold confidence today.

Blessing for Child

God is the creator of everything you see—the beautiful blue sky, babies, friends, animals, and plants. When you see something amazing, don't forget that He is the artist who made it that way. But don't forget that you are one of His very best pieces of art! You're a masterpiece. So stand up straight, smile, and humbly thank Him for all He's given you.

For we are God's *masterpiece*. He has created us *anew* in Christ Jesus, so we can do the good things he *planned* for us long ago.

EPHESIANS 2:10

76

A Faith Adventure

Blessing for Mom

May you follow Jesus to the edges of your comfort zone to get a glimpse of where He's taking you. May you put everything on the table and give Him permission to rearrange your life. May you dare to unclench your fists, look up, and breathe a prayer of thanks right in the midst of this uncertain time, knowing that He's far kinder than you can fathom and far greater than you ever imagined. Can you sense Jesus' invitation to join Him on this adventure of faith? Will you trust Him? Your security is found in Jesus!

Blessing for Child

Be bold for God! Step out in faith and trust that He's got you right where He wants you. Did you know that God wants you to go on exciting adventures with Him? He's just waiting for you to say, "Yes! Let's go!" He'll lead the way and protect you. So take a deep breath, relax, and step out in faith. He's got you!

Without faith it is *impossible*
to please God, because
anyone who comes to him
must *believe* that he exists
and that he rewards those
who *earnestly* seek him.

HEBREWS 11:6 NIV

77

A Wise, Discerning Day

Blessing for Mom

May you be highly discerning in the days ahead! May you know when God is asking you to shore up your faith and stand strong, and when He's inviting you to hide yourself under the shadow of His wing. May you quickly discern the enemy's schemes and stay clear of his traps. In spite of your mistakes, missteps, and misunderstandings, may you never doubt your worth and your value. God will show himself strong in your weakness, faithful in your fears, and merciful where you fall short. Walk wisely with Him today. There's a best place—a best path—for your feet.

Blessing for Child

Dear child, it can sometimes be hard to know right from wrong, or to know what to do and when to do it. May God make you smart, opening your eyes to see what He wants you to see. The devil likes to lay his traps for you, but God can help you see them ahead of time so you can jump right over them as if they weren't even there. Of course, sometimes you'll mess up, but God can forgive you. He loves you and is full of mercy. So walk wisely, knowing how much God loves you.

Do not *conform* to the *pattern* of this world, but be transformed by the *renewing* of your mind. Then you will be able to test and approve what God's will is—his good, pleasing and perfect *will*.

ROMANS 12:2 NIV

78 Believe, Then See

Blessing for Mom

May you walk by faith and not by sight. May you live by the promises of God and not by what your eyes see. May you—even today—see movement in your circumstances, glimpses of glory that remind you God is very much involved in your life. He's writing a story, arranging circumstances, moving in the hearts of people specifically for you. He loves you that much. Let your joyful heart testify to your abounding trust in Him. It'll please God and encourage others!

Blessing for Child

Did you know that sometimes your eyes can play tricks on you? Sometimes something looks good, but it's not, like a yummy apple that has a worm hole on the other side. At other times, things may look bad, but God has a plan to make them good. Maybe you didn't make the team or you got a bad grade—that doesn't mean all is lost. God misses nothing, and He promises to meet you right where you are in this moment. He loves you so much, so trust Him to lead you.

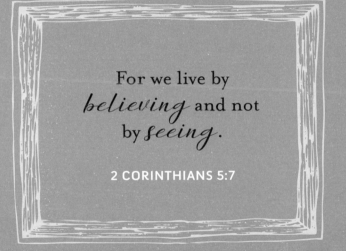

For we live by
believing and not
by *seeing*.

2 CORINTHIANS 5:7

You Can Rely on Him

Blessing for Mom

God is your creator, defender, deliverer, and provider. May He inspire fresh, creative ways to make a living. May He put a fresh spring in your step. May your confidence in Him grow by the moment. May He defend you against the accusations of your critics. May He deliver you from the schemes of the enemy. And may He more than provide for all your needs. He is faithful. Sleep well.

Blessing for Child

Praise God! He gives us everything we need every day. Thank Him for your food, for your house, for your family, for your friends. He protects us from bad people and bad things. Yay, God! He is so good to us. May your eyes open up to all of the good ways God takes care of us. Sleep well knowing He's just like a great big castle that protects you every day.

I will sing of your *strength*,
in the morning I will sing
of your love; for you are my
fortress, my refuge in times of
trouble. You are my strength,
I sing *praise* to you; you,
God, are my fortress, my
God on whom I can *rely*.

PSALM 59:16–17 NIV

80 His Goodness

Blessing for Mom

May you focus more on Jesus' goodness than on your badness. May you get excited about His supply instead of despairing over what you lack in yourself. May you look to Him and imagine what's possible instead of looking down at what seems impossible. God is doing a new thing in your midst. Lean in and look for Him with expectancy today, for every good gift comes from Him, and He loves His children deeply. Choose joy this day!

Blessings for Child

Do you know how good and powerful Jesus is? Look to Him when you feel like you aren't good enough, strong enough, or smart enough. He's good enough for the both of you! He will forgive you for your sins and also give you the strength and encouragement to do amazing things. Everything good comes from Him, and He loves you more than you can know. Smile—He's on your side!

For the LORD God is a *sun* and *shield*; the LORD bestows favor and honor; no good thing does he withhold from those whose walk is *blameless*.

PSALM 84:11 NIV

You're Amazing in Him

Blessing for Mom

May you choose joy today, because in Christ Jesus you are stronger than you know! May you engage your faith today, because God moves when you pray in faith. May you walk confidently today, because Jesus paid a high price for your soul. You matter deeply to Him. May you show compassion today, because you've received such compassion from God himself. You are wrapped up in God's promises, strengthened by His care, and called by His divine will. Everything you need, you already have in Him.

Blessing for Child

May you be so glad about all the great things Jesus has done for you! He helps you be strong, and He listens when you pray to Him. Jesus died on the cross because of how much He loves you—that's how much you matter to Him. When God looks at you, He sees the goodness of His Son, Jesus, in you. He smiles at the thought of you. And He's changing you from the inside out. God has been good to you, so be good to others. You have everything you need in Him. Woo-hoo! Praise God!

The LORD is my *strength*
and *shield*. I trust him
with all my heart. He helps
me, and my heart is *filled*
with joy. I burst out in songs
of *thanksgiving*.

PSALM 28:7

Be Strong, Take Heart

Blessing for Mom

May you refuse to connect the dots on your painful experiences and thus draw a wrong conclusion about yourself and God. May you instead be hemmed in by God's powerful promises, and may you be defined by His very personal love for you. May you refuse to let your past speak to you, except to teach you. And may you insist on living as one who has a redemptive story to tell. You are that important to God's kingdom-story. Walk assured today. God is with you.

Blessing for Child

Sometimes you mess up. Everybody does. But don't let your missteps make you wonder if you are valued and loved. God forgives! He takes bad things and somehow turns them for good. He takes old things and makes them new. You are so important to Him, and He's turning your life into a wonderful story with a happy ending. You are His child! Smile, and be courageous today.

Be *strong* and take heart, all
you who *hope* in the LORD.

PSALM 31:24 NIV

83 Ready to Respond

Blessing for Mom

May God fill you afresh with His Spirit so that you will respond in faith to the smallest nudge within you. May you walk away from time-wasters so that you may possess all God longs to give you. May you turn a deaf ear to lies that "feel true" so you can embrace the beautiful truth that is true! And may God's presence and love be tangible to you today.

Blessing for Child

Are you ready to go where God tells you to go? May your ears hear His voice and your heart be ready to do what He says. It's easy to get distracted, to listen to the wrong voices, and to wander from God's best path for you. When that happens, just stand up, shake yourself off, and talk to God about what He wants you to do and be. His plans for you are your best plans. You can trust Him!

Be dressed *ready* for
service and keep your
lamps *burning*.

LUKE 12:35 NIV

Get Back Up Again

Blessing for Mom

When life knocks you down, may you get back up again because God is mighty in you! When your rogue emotions turn you upside down, may you find your footing again because your Rock is Christ. When the clouds block the sun and your perspective dims, may God himself break through with a fresh reminder of His promises. May the changeable things in your life take a back seat to the unchangeable, never-ending love and faithfulness of God. He has given you a sturdy place to stand.

Blessing for Child

I'm so sorry about what happened. Sometimes we lose the game or get a bad grade. We get sick or someone is really mean to us. Bad things happen, and it's okay to be sad. But remember, your hard times are only temporary. Better days are ahead. And Jesus will always love you! He's the sunshine that breaks through the clouds. He's like a huge, strong rock you can stand on. He told us we'd have some bad days, but He reminded us to cheer up anyway because He has overcome the world. Rise up, dear child! In Christ Jesus, you're stronger than you know.

The godly may *trip*
seven times, but they
will *get up* again.

PROVERBS 24:16

Do Not Fear

Blessing for Mom

When you can't sense what God is up to, may you trust even more His heart toward you. When your journey is different than you would choose, may you see His invitation to make you new. When the storm rages overhead, may you know—with everything in you—that new mercies are on the other side. And when you're tempted to overstate your problems and understate His promises, may you step back and find your footing again. On Christ the solid Rock you stand; all other ground is sinking sand. Embrace a joy-perspective this day!

Blessing for Child

Sometimes it's hard to figure out what's going on. Why do bad things happen? Or why doesn't God come and get you out of your mess right now? Be patient. He's coming! Sometimes we have to go through bad things so we know we're strong enough to face them. Or so we learn to trust Jesus more. But know this—God loves you, and His promises are always true. There's nothing you can trust more than God. So be joyful, knowing a better day is coming!

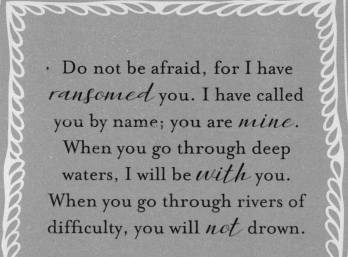

· Do not be afraid, for I have *ransomed* you. I have called you by name; you are *mine*. When you go through deep waters, I will be *with* you. When you go through rivers of difficulty, you will *not* drown.

ISAIAH 43:1–2

Live in Response to Him

Blessing for Mom

May you refuse the autopilot life. May you instead be a lean-in-and-listen kind of person. May you be quick to discern the Lord's whisper and quick to follow His lead. May you notice the winds of change blowing in the trees and loosen your tent stakes if the Lord requires it. And may you cup your ear toward heaven and treasure the Lord's voice above all others. Enjoy your day today!

Blessing for Child

Listen carefully. Can you hear God talking to you? Maybe it's not an "out loud" voice, but a quiet voice in your head telling you what's right and wrong, or what next steps you should take. Sometimes He asks you to change things up—make a new friend or start a new activity. That's great! Don't ignore Him. Pray to Him and read the Bible to learn what He's like and what He wants you to do. God will never steer you wrong! Have a great day.

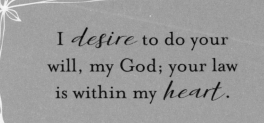

I *desire* to do your
will, my God; your law
is within my *heart*.

PSALM 40:8 NIV

87 A Quiet Place

Blessing for Mom

May you put a high priority on rest and replenishment. May you make a plan to get away and nourish your soul. May you do your work with great excellence. May you take on a challenge that stretches your faith and increases your dependence on God. May your work be especially satisfying and your rest be especially sweet. Life is good that way. Bless you!

Blessing for Child

Sleep is good! God wants us to rest. Yes, enjoy life! But don't be afraid to slow down. It'll fill you back up again. Then you'll show up in life ready for all God has for you! When we're good at resting, it makes us better at other things too. We're better at working and even playing. May you learn to enjoy your downtimes. And may you have sweet, restful sleep tonight and a great day tomorrow.

Then, because so many people were coming and going that they did not even have a chance to eat, [Jesus] said to them, "*Come* with me by yourselves to a quiet place and get some *rest*."

MARK 6:31 NIV

Have a Brave Day

Blessing for Mom

May you be a tender-teachable Christ-follower and respond to God's invitation to make you more like Him. Whenever He calls you up, it means He's getting ready to call you out to a new place, a new assignment, and a new land of promise. Refuse the enemy's taunts. Respond to the Guardian of your soul. He loves you and intends to use you greatly. Have a brave day.

Blessing for Your Child

Dear child, always be humble and ready to learn from Jesus. He has big plans for you and wants you to have wonderful adventures with Him. Don't listen to the devil—he sounds like fun sometimes, but he's just going to drag you down. He doesn't love you. God does! Remember how much He loves you, and be brave for God!

Once you were like sheep who *wandered* away. But now you have turned to your Shepherd, the Guardian of your *souls*.

1 PETER 2:25

Pray Audaciously, Obey Immediately

Blessing for Mom

May Jesus himself open your eyes to His activity on the earth today. May God give you insight into others' stories so you will know what to say and when to say it. Instead of looking too long at the enemy's wicked schemes, remember this: Whenever the devil makes a move, God already has a plan, and His purposes WILL prevail. Pray audaciously. Obey immediately. God has you on the earth today for a reason. May He find faith in you. Blessings on your day today.

Blessing for Child

Can you see what God is doing? It's so exciting to watch Him move. May God open up your eyes to all the great stories He's writing in the lives of your friends and family. That way you'll know what to say and do! The devil wants to mess things up, but God will win the day. He always does. Pray big, brave prayers! Then obey God and watch what He'll do. Be blessed today.

Listen, stay *alert*, stand tall in the faith, be *courageous*, and be *strong*.

1 CORINTHIANS 16:13 THE VOICE

90

Jesus Loves You

Blessing for Mom

No matter what you're going through, may you know in the depths of your soul that you are loved. Your identity is completely secure. It's not up for grabs or changeable with popular opinion. Jesus loves how He made you! Seasons come and seasons go, but God's love for you never changes. It is abundant, profound, and amazingly real, right here, right now. Walk like you're loved, because you are, beyond your wildest dreams. Have a beautiful day!

Blessing for Your Child

Jesus loves you. Never forget that. He loves you so much that He died for you. You have nothing to fear, nothing to be ashamed of. It doesn't matter what anyone else says about you—God made you exactly the way He wanted you to be. And His love NEVER changes. It is a huge, amazing, deep love that's beyond your craziest dreams. Have a beautiful day!

May you experience the *love* of Christ, though it is too great to understand fully. Then you will be made *complete* with all the fullness of life and power that *comes* from God.

EPHESIANS 3:19

ACKNOWLEDGMENTS

Confession. This book was not my idea. The vision for this project came from my dear friend and editor, Andy McGuire (who happens to write and illustrate children's books on the side). Given the vitriolic nature of our culture and the power of the spoken word, Andy pondered what it might look like to take some of my blessings and rework them to speak over our children. Together, Andy and I wrote the children's blessings, and I served as editor this time. I think we've come up with a book that will bring life to your family and stir up faith in both you and your children. We sure pray so. May God bless you as you speak life over your family.

SUSIE LARSON (www.susielarson.com) is a national speaker, bestselling author, and the host of the daily talk show *Susie Larson Live*, heard on the Faith Radio Network. Susie has written eighteen books and many articles. She's been a guest on *Focus on the Family*, *The Life Today Show*, *Family Life Today*, and many other media outlets. Voted twice as a top-ten finalist for the John C. Maxwell Transformational Leadership Award, she is also a veteran of the fitness field. Susie has been married to her dear husband, Kevin, since 1985, and together they have three wonderful sons, three beautiful daughters-in-law, three beautiful grandchildren, and one adorable pit bull named Memphis. Susie's passion is to see people everywhere awakened to the value of their soul, the depth of God's love, and the height of their calling in Christ Jesus. May his face shine upon you.